T0357929

INSIDE OUT
WAKEFIELD PRESS

Tasmanian by birth and upbringing, Syd Harrex lives in Adelaide where he is Reader in English and Director of the Centre for Research in the New Literatures in English at Flinders University. His first poetry collection, *Atlantis and Other Islands*, was runner-up for the Commonwealth Poetry Prize and a British Book News Shortlist selection. An extensively-published critic and scholar, his other works include *The Fire and the Offering: The English-language Novel of India 1935-1970* (Vol 1 1977, Vol 11 1978); *Only Connect: Literary Perspectives East and West* (1981); *Kamala Das* (1986); *R.K. Narayan, A Story-teller's World* (1989); *The Green Prodigals: Contemporary Stories and Poems from Korea* (1989); and *Companions of Pilgrimage* (forthcoming, Washington 1991).

Inside Out

SYD HARREX

Wakefield Press

Wakefield Press
43 Wakefield Street
Kent Town
South Australia 5067

First published 1991

Cover image by Tom Gleghorn
Typeset and text design by Katy Hasenohr
Printed by Hyde Park Press
4 Deacon Avenue, Richmond, SA 5033

Made and printed in Australia

Promotion of this title has been assisted by the South
Australian Government through the Department for the
Arts and Cultural Heritage.

Creative writing program assisted by the Australia Council,
the Australian Government's arts funding and advisory body.

ISBN 1 86254 269 4

Author's Note

I have pleasure in acknowledging my indebtedness to Gwen Harwood, Graham Rowlands and Michael Bollen for their constructive comments concerning the manuscript, and to Katy Hasenohr for her professional preparation of it for the publisher. I am immensely grateful to Tom Gleghorn whose painting, created especially for this book, graces its cover.

I also wish to acknowledge the periodicals in which some of the poems in this collection first appeared: *The Adelaide Review* ('Crossing Yeats's O'Connell Street', 'Sporting Fixture', 'Surmising India', 'Was It Just a Bee?'); *Ariel* ('The Pleasures of Being an Outsider'); *The Australian* ('Echocardiogram'); *Island* ('Inside Out'); *Poetry Australia* ('Beatrice Islets Conservation Park'); *Quadrant* ('All a Green Willow', 'Laundry Window', 'An August Front'); and *Span* ('Walking Out in the Clare Valley', 'Jamaican Journal').

Poems

Echocardiogram

*"Fool", said my Muse to me, "look into thy heart
and write".*

Sir Philip Sidney

I have just seen my heart
on a screen:
black and white, dim and blurred,
with ventricles, arteries, valves,
curving walls and worm walls,
pulsing images from left to right
like little cathedrals on wheels,
surreal recesses
where dreams and sacred
knowledge disappear
and I know not what I see.

Yet of this I am sure:
there was no figure there
to name Passion,
no Poetry,
no Mystery even
to the trained observer.
My heart is only a pumping
station, unattended.

But, Jesus,
it doesn't half work.

Walking Out in the Clare Valley

i
The morning gate is shut
but if you
don't open it
and walk out

the hour does anyway,
and after it the day.

i i
The distance between
one step and the next
is a length of charred bark
that was snatched
from a passing tree.

i i i
Yellow and orange irises
lodged in olive flesh
return my fixed stare:

more wild flowers
in the October bush
than my poor pupils,
may ever number, ever sight.

iv
Don't speak,
not even to yourself;
so delicious the birds'
tones, their music:
despise commentary.

v
Fields full of grass
like green wool
ready to be sheared
by knitting sheep.

vi
A large log
across your path
invites you to sit
a while and rest
between stanzas.

Like your last footsteps,
your thoughts are melting...

vii
Plovers squabble,
crows are shrill
and garrulous,
but kookaburras
just laugh out their name
over and over.

viii
The cathedrals of Europe
gothic in their beauty,
final in their pronouncements;

yet put one here amid
the blue ranges and ochre ridges,
how confident then
its answers to the oldest
questions this country asks?

ix
Two boys on bitser bikes
ride through my riddles
leaving me to recoup
what truth I can

like their dust
in my watering eyes.

x
The bush cottage
and vine-row oils,
the watercolour hints
of floating hills,

are not the only spring
exhibits: charcoal sketches
from last summer's ashes
still arrest the eye:

fragments of black bones
scattered in weeds and sky.

xi
Picture in four months' time
in the dry brown weather
the wind a belting door
on hot screaming hinges,
the perforating rasp of sheep
rattling thick herds of dust,
the creek with nothing, nothing to say.

xii

Despite the savagery of fire,
the land and its animals'
black and smoking carcasses,
the ritual of renewals
is secure as the sun is secure.

Winter rains raise the word
of death to speech of seed and leaf;
the single human has only one
life's chance of being heard.

xiii

So I think I can't imagine
the nuclear winter they say
we are threatened by
even here where the fat sun
grazes like a munching cow
in a froth of poppies,
and eucalypts shimmer into song.

But suddenly I shudder
in my tracks, stopped by an idea
that all I breathe,
touch, taste, see, hear,
is only magic waiting to vanish,
as men ordain,
in everlasting death.

xiv
Flames love the fat
of the land, its wheat fur,
when the bush is a lather
of heat and sweats buckets
like broken-in horses.

Then if a wind rises
out of the north's oven
carrying a single spark,
the Lord promises
black judgement.

xv
There is also slow decaying wood
feathered with fungus and moss
which did not burn;

a peace so prevailing
that makes fire even
seem unaccomplished.

xvi
In the ploughed paddocks:

great gums recently uprooted
by machines like giant ants,
by metal men like robots.

All that remains
of their forest power,
like toppled towers
on the pile of history,
is the fading traction
of a lost message.

xvii
Sun disperses
bush filters
blood-trickling light;

earth on which you walk
is a cushion of cool shade.

Everything near you expands
into the mystery of itself,
except for your own shadow
stretching
disappearing
beyond who you are...

xviii
The wending valley lingers
in its dusk which peels in places
where window panes and
tilting poles brier lights.

Do those who nurture here
see the fruits of gladness,
a beacon name like *God*,
sculptured in their porches?

Their planter ancestors
of the riesling vineyards
were also pickers
of the Bible's metaphors.

xix
Vineyards on hillsides
wineries in hollows
orchards in pastures
gardens in orchards
go forth and multiply...

dirt roads and lanes
plank and rock bridges
stone and wooden houses
weatherboard churches
stone and slate churches
go forth and multiply...

xx
Here in this sooner age
I am content
with the wine
from the bottle,
gold from the green
red from the brown;

an occasional simile
for the grace and miracle
of the crushed grape
saved for the palate;

and leave the myths
where they belong
to autumn on the vines:
subsumed, secret,
in their perpetual song.

All a Green Willow

A boy's year like mine
had just two seasons:
Aussie Rules and Cricket.

The discovery of girls
and swimming after tennis
also glowed with summer good,

but the time on which I gloat
is saturated by the smell
of linseed oil in willow wood.

Rich then and complex now
the leather rush of red, the race
across the stain of green:

they helped me read a poem's
beauty through, see its stumps of birth
and death, with life running in-between.

Black Magic

Remember when luxury
was a box of chocolates
or a packet of Players
before you were old enough
for your first wallet?
And adventure was a tram ride
rocking along tracks that sped
straight through the Wild West?

And summer holidays
were a white shack at the beach
other families motored down
to (you always drove 'up'
to town and 'down' the river)
in dented red Prefects
or black carnivorous Buicks?

Why didn't we save those comics—
Superman, Comic Cuts, Dick Tracy,
Ginger Megs, Classic Comics
(remember that White Whale?)—the shop
got in each Thursday, and sold out
of (except the *True Romances*
that made you spew) as soon
as you raced your bikes from school
the mile down-hill, first in
first cuts?

Nothing could equal
the paper and print smell
when the pages opened like Eden
for the first time. Swaps
and second-hands had always
lost that first and last fragrance;
all innocence, violence, surprise
betrayed by other tongues,
eaten by other eyes.

End of Indian Summer

i
Last week shorts:

legs long as adolescent love
retaining their ritual tan
in the hot elastic light;

such a bonus of surplus sun,
such a lazy retarded autumn
swollen with campus girls;
their motherhood spared, remote.

i i
This week jeans:

the summer juice of gorgeous peaches
forgotten now in each silken throat
warmed by winding wool of scarves

as the chill like a knife
peels and slices the hard dark fruit
of winter air in wet trees.
Wombs are now prepared for life.

An August Front

Across the gulf, sly change
whiting out the sky.
Warm airs retreat to die
in the quarried sea-sawn range

of residential hills.
Trees enrage the wind:
branches broken, birds pinned,
by catapulting wills.

Blood and stone the mix
of weathers, a higher force,
as if nuptial and divorce
depend on the same crucifix.

Wait, then, for a different sign,
devoid of pain; a climate
of love and not of hate.
May a mist of sunshine

gather all you hold:
the daffodil plunder
as you climb from under
the wattle's heights of gold.

Mother and Son

The moon citadels
spout milk
down their slopes.

Birds spill
songs of chaos
from the sun-

splashed trellises.
The babe's mouth
locks up the flow

of silver love
and churns it
into secret gold.

Aussie in London

From his country of steaks and wine
back to the land of ties and suits,
dismayed by his dollar's decline
he refines his culture-pursuits.

He dines on frugal sandwiches
and cultivates the Art of Walk,
is shrewd in everything he says
in case there's VAT on talk.

With student card from Istanbul
he lives again his Uni days,
disrobing damsels in his skull
while watching existential plays.

He specialises in Scot-free
seeing St Paul's outside only,
thinks aloud while coaxing a pee
to prove he is never lonely.

Says he: "It's time to go to Rome",
but sinks the plan boozed on Guinness
for a spiced, gum-tree flash of home;
a far trembling in his penis.

Was It Just a Bee?

And there was the Globe
day-dream drifting.
Under that Southwark roof
Hamlet succumbed to poison
and Bottom to the brewery
passion of his fart:
these, the mortal extremes
of Shakespeare's art.

Out of the sunless air
across my casement
swaggers an insect
which looks like a bee,
yet doesn't buzz like one.
Soon I see it has yellow stripes,
giving it the semblance
of a fop gone to fat...

Where am I? Surely
not already at Eastcheap
in the Boar's Head Tavern?

This Falstaff of the fat fly
species, mead-intoxicated
and flapping erratically
in ever-decreasing circles,
would hedge me in.
"Go, prithee go, your Queen
Tearsheet craves thee", I say,
bowing, scraping, pushing him
back over the battlement.

Pray he find a merry hive
to deposit his surfeit of honey-lard,
and may his royal fare dismiss him
with that coldest of greetings:
"I know thee not, old man".

Whence my visitant dissolved,
melted into air like the Globe,
while I wake back to cakes and ale
and wonder if my vision
was a beer-allergic fever,
a neurotic synchronicity even,
or was it just a bee?

Crossing Yeats's O'Connell Street

(for Janet Wilson)

Half way across
the red light halts us
at the median strip.

Time to watch
a pavement artist
chalking down the Holy

Virgin's eyes; time
to hear some Crazy Jane
(an idol in her stabbing

hand) babbling incantations
to the swollen heavens.
Time for Dublin mysticism

until the traffic-light
flashes WALK WALK WALK.
The lame obey, we hurry on.

The spell is snapped like a spine.

Jamaican Journal

So my island drifts
plundered by butterflies.
The dog lifts his mourning to heaven.
Edward Kamau Brathwaite

I *saturday 31 Oct*

(Ref)Rain in the two Kingston Towns

when is this rain this rain
to abate abate this biblical rain
this water explosion
this jamaican noah's
rain's rain...

this deluge dialect
i can't translate
this patois beat
i can't explain
out of the instinct
of my island home,
of the rains sewn
in its volcanic earth
and black shining bone
(rock o roughly round
in the sling
of the roaring forties)?

rains we wore like garden
or household garments

each of a different weave:
winter's cloak of ice-stiff blades,
spring's hoof-print falls,
summer's rainbow sunshowers,
soft steam of autumn drippage...

but of what use this atlas
know-how of tasmanian weather
in this other huger kingston town?
(useless i guess as fire
embracing ice, and feste's
rain won't explain at all
equator or antipodes)...

when is this rain
this   rain!!!!!!!!!!
to abate
abate???????????
this biblical
jamaican
noah's
rain's
raining
to abate?!?!?!?!?!
abate?!?!?!?!?!?!?

WHEN WILL IT BLOODY WELL STOP?

II *tuesday 3 Nov*

the star-sized light
between reef-black sea
and grey ore of clouds
on the red bar of sunset

is a Florida liner
which arrowed out of dock
a humid hour ago

III *wednesday 4 Nov*

Walking the Waterfall at Ocho Rios
(for Wilson Harris)

i
Today we climbed Dunn's River Falls.
We linked white hands in a chain gang
led by Johnny, a black guide whose name
is red on his t-shirt green.
Johnny carries our possessions (handbags,
cameras, sunglasses, shirts, watches,
purses) and he averts disasters.
Some graze superfluous flesh,
others slip and slide, all splash,
wounds are trivial, and Johnny teaches
us all to walk up falling rivers.
There are wooden stairs and platforms
alongside rapids and twisting torrents
for tourists to watch the tourist climbers.
After the final purifying ascent
to the river's highest horizontal course
we bathe our bones, wash out our sneakers.
What does it mean, this climb
against gravity up ropes of water,
other than a baptism of physical pleasure?
Is it a fake triumph, does anyone wonder,
an illusion that people are links
in a chain of love and brotherhood?

ii
There's refreshment at the Falls Bar
where a black singer sweet-talks
a microphone that perches on a stack
of *Red Stripe* cardboard boxes.
He sings the smoky melodies
of Hogie Carmichael and Nat King Cole.
An obese Stars-&-Stripes couple seize
the image: she poses kissing-distance
from the singer's blues-shaped lips; *slick*!
her husband snaps them in a frame
for their album mantlepiece in Indiana.
Then they depart in sensitive haste,
ignoring the singer's collection box.
They know ol' bluesman don't know
he posed for their photograph,
for he's blind you see.

iii
We had climbed a waterfall
as a labour of ecstasy:
we were rewarded with the song
of the blind and cold beer:
we had ring-side seats
at a cheap exhibition
of disgraced compassion:
could anything sanctify this?

Alone, the song-maker
suffers his blindness bliss.

iv
So that was the meaning of the day:
a masquerade of community
in a world of moral disappearances
like the pleasure cruiser's lights
in the horizon's final flames.
That was all....
                            But then a flash
of recall, a fusing of exertions,
a truth of coincidences perhaps:
I see, Wilson, your double-death Donne's
floating ascension through waterfall hair
and his blind eye seeing again
in a world of re-enactments;
see and hear you unblinding
the song, unsaying the wrong
of the unascending fall,
syllable by dissolving syllable....

So is it you who says and asks:
the symbol is never what it seems
have you been chosen by the wrong word?

IV *saturday 7 Nov*

**Passing Through Passport Control at
Kingston Airport You Never Looked Back**

That matted white Mexican hat
with the red cranium band,
no I didn't fall for surreptitious that
left on my pillow, you understand.
(*I made you wear it out of sight.*)

And when from a shaking bus returned
Down Town, and a cab back to the lick
of lonely rum you had abandoned,
and how about that sipping lipstick
(*you wear it out of sight*)

kissing the dimpled plastic glass
still trembling in the hand
of your departure? Yes, that's class!
I guess you guess I understand
(*as you fling your hat out of sight*).

As did I when raining slashed the sky
and you grave-gripped my going hand.
The black clouds here still tumble by
while you are landing in another land...
(*and I see your hat surging into sight*).

V *tuesday 10 Nov*

lovers engulfed all night
pulsing on the tide
cast their death away
on drifting starlight

see the lemon butterfly
afloat in liquid light:
the new day's filament
of love that burned all night

VI *wednesday 11 Nov*

Jamaican Nights

Very soon a dog will bark
and then a mongrel orchestra
will salivate-salivate out of tune
over old bone juicy moon;
far and late, sly the dark
will eat and rot another star.

Very soon bad dreams will start.
A walking dead turns born
again in a sleeping heart,
father to a forgetful son
who wakes in sweat from siren blows,
from fascist squads of mosquitoes.

So the pattern flows and cracks,
same rum-laced nightmares but guiltier:
a distant bush's retracing tracks
leading here to crimes beneath the palms,
the hurting past, tropic connecting winter,
and no love cradling in his arms.

VII *friday 13 Nov*

Acts of Violence

knife in the park
X's answer to question Y
throat of a nature lover
zipped open in the dark

i
How can we understand
the violence of that hand?
How ignore the midnight hiss
while we stroll by in light?

Surely no one wants to meet
a mad machete in the dark
not even as a rite of bliss
for a fatally broken heart.

i i
From the garden's labyrinths
were heard staccato shots
in the unofficial civil war.
Inked police arrive, spread like blots.

Morning's independent witness
calibrates the weapon's bore,
the victim's prowess in his pain.
Yes, Gethsemane again, again.

The martyr's t-shirt wore
Blood Rain Blood Rain
and the only killer they detain
is innocent once more.

VIII *saturday 14 Nov*

Mosquitoes

Smaller than Australian mosquitoes,
therefore harder to CLAP-SMASH
in hand or shoot with spray,
the Jamaican variety display
Anancy mastery of underhand
play more diabolical even than
the Chappells' cricket brand.

Being the insects they are, of course,
they don't respect privacy
but to make matters worse
they enter any pore or orifice

at any time of night or day,
despite clear signs like
EXECUTIVE PERSONNEL ONLY.
They don't whine their warnings
out of any sense of fair play,
but to bring you insomnia:
thousands of conscious seconds
to admire their mosquito mastery
of psychological warfare
and subtle torture
until you see the light.

And yet, as with all malevolent
creatures, their evil is relative.
Jamaican mosquitoes do have
their small-mercy better sides:
for instance, they don't
inject you with malaria,
yellow fever, or elephantiasis.

And they buzz a moral, too, which is:
Wakeful and Thankful be for This.

IX *sunday 15 Nov*

Sporting Fixture
(University of the West Indies, Mona)

Slap against the bricks, tattered figure in cricket cap,
     shirt,
jeans and sandshoes (the sport of life's renegade attire)

patiently poses, lassitude and poverty in collusion, but
     look
again and the cartoon too contains lines like
     Michelangelo's.

Reggae Stars, Calypso Kings, Cricket Greats, have folk-
     hero
names like Half Pint, Mighty Sparrow, and Supercat, so

why not him too in his occupation of holding up a wall?
He's a hero in his leaning way there by the window day
     on day;

limp and loose of posture (muscles tuned and so relaxed
I've never yet quite caught him out changing stance),

right shoulder to the wall, left hand on hip, legs ankles-
     crossed,
he's dead spit of the great fast bowler in a photograph

scrutinising the trenchant umpire's fallibility.
What has he done to me, this faceless figure who does
     not know me,

that I waste this Sunday mesmerised at my window
with a back view of his black mystery? Excluded
     member

of the audience, he peers through the grill into the
        raucous
room of thrills, screams, disasters, tragedies, choking
        laughter

and watches every flash and flicker of every programme
in the Student TV Lounge. There he leans, there he
        stands,

until bad light only, never rain, stops play.
I wish I could give him at least a name to gather

in his anonymous fame, a title to honour
his great colonial waiting game...call him *Sporting*
        Fixture.

X *thursday 3 Dec*

here the island picture
like the road's bend
is ever incomplete

truth and beauty
such a jungle mixture

what beginning and what end?
only sea seems complete

The Pleasures of Being an Outsider
(Cave Hill, Barbados)

A man is always resident in the castle of his skin. If the castle is deserted, then we know the Devil has been at work.

George Lamming

i
Not all of you just gives the tourist's due:
cash transactions. A gift-wrapped invasion
of feeling, some qualified point of view,
are gestures from choice, not obligation.
Tacit as a hand-shake, polite torpor
enjoys equality with friendliness.
Bajan joy and anger are not your lore,
nor their history your slave business.
Aloneness is sanctuary, place of play
like a cool courtyard pool on a hot day;
a skin of ripples where your past may float
revealed, free of mud, as you have made it:
where blood-stained petals of inheritance
and stamen swans of love drift forth their dance.

ii
Sky and earth contest, a hawk arbitrates.
Here   tension of wings made hammock light   is
floating radiance ... fraternity of water
(rain-riding rivers reaching oceans), fire's
cycle of cannibalism, of death and haloes,
composts smouldering with life. Birth begins
with satiation in search of hunger;
the rest is mixture, rival ratios.
The predatory bird unites, anoints.
Fish feeds on fish to prepare your banquets.
Your polka-dot eyes scan the moon's strip-tease
in clouds, endless milky space, galaxies,
until your being trembles like thunder
pondering the torture of true wonder.

iii
Itinerant exile on this sugar isle
of breezes (whose mantle is Ariel
set free to relish his rite of passage)
where Caliban's laureate lives at Hotel
Atlantis in the town of Bathsheba
(a rocks-and-beach stroll to Cattlewash but
a moon's throw from menstrual Africa),
has any man asked you into his hut?
Delight in clean sea-winds, wooden houses
painted to butterfly the crush of trees,
delight the sun dance in human voices,
surf drums from th'Atlantic's orchestra pit.
But remember, Visitor and Others,
face to face you may be futile mirrors.

iv

You lounge upstairs, sipping fiction and rum;
some flamboyant Guyanese fiasco
set against savannahs of fatalism.
You sink in syrup of despair. Below,
professors normally quiet and slow
thump-jump the table with their dominoes,
the stakes high—rounds of beers and ego blows.
Nor book nor drink serve what you need to know.
Outside, the wave-shaped passion of the wind
in long grass, the durable shell of blue
sky, the cricket captain placing his field,
the sun and sport of pleasure's revenue,
all enrich the day, hail the rhythmical.
Why is such simple life so mystical?

Laundry Window

Laundry windows seldom afford
such a view: a hill
Hawaiians call the Sleeping God,
and a girl gardening
as if in prayer,
bending over pegged plants
like nappies on a line.

Though the day is storm-blown
she has fixture status
like the snoring deity of stone.
What would she say ("absurd"?)
if she knew she was filling
my mind as a bird
perched on a bare bough
can fill the eye at sunset?
Contact is like that,
the knowing and the unknowing
meeting like flesh and bone:
this window frame that puts her there.

I plunge my hands back in the suds
and rinse my lurid underwear.

Never Has It Been So Neat
(to Susan leaving for India)

Never has it been so neat, your desk,
tidied now like a paddock
after the harvest has been cut and bundled;
"such a crop of hay as never!"
and what price those lost quotations
coming to hand and mind again?

Now like the sun, old discoverer, I see
things we never knew were there,
nostalgic as pre-decimal coins and stamps:

this row of reference works between
card-index trunks, that box file stack,
these photocopied essays guillotine-
manicured, stapled, numbered; IN-
TRAY spilling inwards instead of over,
your *Invicta* calendar visible at last,
albeit open anachronistically at the day
last month (Tuesday 8 August) which advises

most people sell their souls and live
with a good conscience on the proceeds
                    —Smith;

foreign envelopes, correspondence, newsletters,
journals, three books flagged with paper
markers—good soldiers all—standing at ease
until you return commanding *atten-shun!*

a nuclear family of ornamental elephants
fingered into a casual regimen as if to concede
holiday's rhythm, Indian possibilities;
and—not seen in years—naked square inches
of the cup-ringed, blotched, faded wood veneer
the desk top is still made of after all.
Like the lonely echo of a forgotten call.

Surmising India
(for K. Ayyappa Paniker)

I Elephanta

i
Sculptors carved a cosmos
in the cave. After that
they quietly chiselled
three Shivas in One.

Being cautious craftsmen
they also left tough pillars
to the roof—just in case
Eternity needs propping up.

i i
If ever human arm
were turned to stone
who would not wish
his to be as Shiva's
enfolding Parvati?

and who not wish
hers to be the bosom
that gives to God's hand
a lover's igniting touch?

iii
But when the colonisers came
God was no more than a bull's-eye.

The Portuguese for sport
and target-practice
blasted to fragments
the first Shiva they saw

forgetting that a God's son
needs no lingam to seed
with, nor legs nor feet to walk on.

II Airport

The sky is white
blinding tarmac:

saris are boarding
the Boeing
upside down.

III 'Heat and Dust'

Before the monsoon
the hot season
cancels all verbs;

hearts spill dust.

IV Still Life Breakfasts

i
After a morsel of minutes
sliced from burning time
the fresh bread
is crisp as toast.

Stiff upper-lipped,
the moustached marmalade
has not waited in vain.

ii
I went to Tamil Nadu
to see the rope trick
but had no luck

then one morning
in a dak bungalow
while I wasn't looking

the yellow plantains
unpeeled themselves
for my entertainment.

V Kovalum Bus Stop

I wait under a sun-pecked
shelter of leaves, shaded
by fool's motley.
I ask, "What time the bus
to Trivandrum?"
Faces grin forth
answers like bananas.
Eyes stare back timetables
uselessly untranslated.

Only the village cripple
treats me as an approximate
equal till he too is bored
by the digital watch
that still cuffs my wrist somehow,
reminding me I'm late.

I have my waiting choices now—
panic or resignation—
but opt for the latter
knowing you are infinitely patient
but that Kamala, who once slapped
the moon's face, will be somewhat
larger than love,

and that one night the moon too
must dissolve forever in silver sleep,
and the blue sky will never need to know.

Five Tamil Flowers for Sudesh Mishra

I Kurinci

Where the snow-birds melt in summer's arms
two loves twine on mountain air.
He picks the white kurinci flowers
and plucks pine-needles from her hair.

II Mullai

Wait dear, patiently: from the forest
I shall bring jasmine of desire.
Go to the pastures where egrets feed
and gather dung cakes for our fire.

III Marutam

Like the monsoon, the Queen's flower burns
in dalliance and rains too late
torrents on my fields. To Him her rice
of love, to me an empty plate.

IV Neytal

This seashore is a place of skeletons;
I am coral in the tide.
You, blue lily, drift on the oceans.
Your heart is where I cannot bide.

V Palai

They eloped at length to the wasteland,
and came to the desert tree;
old parents—Life, Death—were left behind.
Their ashes bloomed, their eyes could see.

Kangaroo Island Sketches

I The Ferry Arriving

Quick lines of sketching in a book
push like veins, pull like wires,

until the puppet shape resembles
the breaching manoeuvre of arrival;

then the ferry berths tied to its match-stick
jetty, and fixes into a toy of itself:

slips of sight your study reassembles;
a painting perhaps lopsided on a hook.

II Paint Brushes

On a red table
in front of the window—
a glass bowl with brushes
sticking out of Indian
ink stained water.

And this indigo
liquid becomes the sea
the window holds
in its glass.

And those
black brushes in the bowl
were painted here
by these black brushes in the bowl.

III Beatrice Islets Conservation Park

Between clumped rocks like lumps of coal,
and the sea plain (its dark pastures
of kelp, its rubber crops), remnants
of crooked fence cross the slack mud.

You sit in a whisked hide of reeds,
sketching a pair of cormorants
perched on adjacent knock-kneed poles.
Their linear incidence of tails,

grey backs, black-rimmed white-masked faces,
make a perfect pose, and you're sure
the propping boats, pendulum parks
of sea-bed sand, the Bay of Shoals

flanked by straw hills north to Cape Rouge,
can be etched in later. But birds
are unpredictable, a whim
of wings; so is accuracy

of painter's hand and poet's eye.
Your pencil breaks, the cormorants
fly free of frames, while in their place
remain warped traces of their grace.

IV Near Willson's River, Mouth Flat

A sea mist softly pricks our flesh.
The rollers, successive, concussive, break:
luminous lime, exploding snow
in the flame of the summer day.

The yellow beach is rifted with white,
a milky way of shells, grit and bones.
The honeycomb cliffs, indented with caves
of mustard sand, powder to gold

as the sun's last rays level horizontal
and gulls unstitch the silver from the sky.
This is a place where homo sapiens pleasures
are still confined to random footprint measures.

V Near Windmill Beach, Cape Willoughby

How sunlight is varnished by moist sea air
late summer day dying gathering grain
as of planed pinewood, the solid, the doomed
earth, how floating, roaming in sky it is;
frail seeming its boulders of inflated
bladders, cliffs of collapsed cardboard boxes,
how like cinema sets, illusion blink-
ing just in the eye of the beholder.
Space appears stasis yet all is action,
orange rust on rocks, engines of ocean
pounding tunnels into coasts, fireworks foam.
How tenuous, trifling, this my life-time:
human story expunged like esplanades
of stars, mutated from four elements....

VI Summer Snapshots At Hog Bay

i
Dappled collage of winter
cream and ray-lamp tan,
annual hedonists of the sun
prostrate their oiled bodies
in sport with beach, sea, wind, fire.

i i
Elders, mothers of toddlers,
mindful of heat's malice,
sit on black squares of sand
under striped canvas awnings
dyed blue/white green/white cool.

i i i
Zoom in on the rituals of play:

i v
wind-surfing triangles
like coralescent fins;
bat-n-ball games; wrists
dressing the breezes with kites
in diamond dog-fights;

v
carnal stares behind dark glasses
inspecting bikinis like tropical
fish in a tank, ivory lozenges
of unwrapped breasts slyly
licked by tongues of ultra violet...

v i
and Camera Eye   ace of voyeurs
back   boxed in his dark room
rinsing reality into being   squinting
at these his negative transparencies,
and pegging prints on a line.

VII Autumn Nostalgia

Grey April light, silver stabbing through clouds,
the sea's creases, day dressed in gull colours,
fortunate fishing weather in Hog Bay,
hands on nylon lines in touch with death
in the making, the higher creature God
to the lower, the winds' whispers and words
tepid from the island's secret places.
A message coded in breeze and grass. Birds
read It; wallabies—ears erect—smell It.
But man, who can't trust himself, can only
hunger Revelation as nostalgia:
the past's emotion of the future, night
stranger tapping a door, and quaver-tone
memory's garden once upon a life-time.

VIII Libran Birthday

In ivory winds like these, whip-handled,
off the shining flanks of the bucking mare
(pun: honour of Baudin), this chopped
crystal of waters given the sinister
map name *Backstairs Passage*;

these breezes threshing into Hog Bay by
bouncing trawlers tethered to the pier,
this blue tremor in ear-shaped shells
some fancy is a sea-soul's pain;
this gale of mixed seasons green

now as it fuses with the island Spring,
convulsion or tantrum of a dark angel's
symphony, its paper score torn
into scraps of seagulls; this crush of air,
this writhing botany planted or

uprooted; froth of wild-flowers
in a surf of grasses (bluewinged
Comesperma; Epacris impressa
cathedral bells; purple
sneezing spasms of *Swainsona*);

this air-borne honey of fertility
spilling cells of seeds wherever,
this fever fore and aft history
that blew the burnt Europeans here
in their moth-winged match-stick ships—

Investigator, Le Geographe, Casuarina—
and us long-weekending on this shore
white-laced with foam: we charge
these winds to enfold in tissue of gold
your first birthday here in Penneshaw.

IX Antechamber Bay
(for Christopher Koch)

We took the graded road that slides
by spartan farms and mallee bush
to Chapman River where surf-tides
year about disturb the tannin

ti-tree water and brackish bream
trapped like time from Lashmar Lagoon
to the beach (where it's safe to swim)
which arcs the bay for five white miles.

We walked the short northern end
from what should have been the river
mouth. Child summers you used to spend
at Swansea many moons from Wales

were texts redrawn by the placid
lines and hues of Antechamber's
shores which passed your subtle acid
test concerning littoral beauty—

sun-filed sea; bushes, grass and trees
in jigsaw patterns to present
the total range of greens with ease
gripped or smudged by tawny russets.

You named the landscape parallels
with the East Coast of Tasmania:
the mirror air, the sand-dune swells,
and splashes here and there of wine;

delicacies to paint in soft
watercolours' true elusive
tones rather than, as from aloft,
with assertive impasto oils.

It seems inevitable now
we should have stolen from that scene
something rare like a golden bough—
something more than sheer impressions.

So it was. We dug from the beach
strange florid tubers you planted
later in my garden sand. Six
weeks have passed, soursobs roam, and yet

two of three still live. We wonder
if they're toothbrush Calothamnus,
and chance a hunch—come spring plunder—
these plants will flame their name at us.

Inside Out

By day
the wide window lets in light
to paint the room exactly as it is,

sees us look out to the terraced sea,
itching the frayed shore, exactly as it is;
            but now at night the wintry
glass is mirror as well as pane,
confusing one lens of reality
with another (rather like two reels
of a film projected simultaneously),
for that's exactly as it is.

Looking out
we first sight our reflected selves
spying back into the familiar webs
in which we arrange our lives...
            an office-lamp,
the Coonawarra wine bottle
with a candle stuck in its neck, wick black,
encrusted with wax like grains of rice,
a pyramid of lemons, mandarins, pears, oranges
on a grape-fruit base in a big ceramic
bowl,   baroque bananas beside
a net of brown onions—all on the kitchen bar
like an authentic *Still Life*;
            the mounted poster, *Irish Pub Signs*,
which hangs on the back wall next to the fridge;
            the crockery and pantry cabinet (its
upper storey lead-lighted like a low-church chancel,
or a bay window in a stainless B & B street)
denouncing opposite   *that*

archaeological artist's reconstruction
(photo-copied) of a Minoan Knossos fresco
(to be exact, the Bull Wrestlers
on a blue background); &
          the hard fact on which I am writing,
this red dining-table.

Yet
we also look out, seeing out,
through the same picture in the same frame,
noticing the far furry lights
of the Mainland where birth and death
really live; the moonlit strait
of floating stars to the east of our island jetty's
sole beacon pulsing its sign
of who's here, of who wants to be known;
          and just two feet from the window
amidst sinister insects in the garden
that's clamour to the eye, the drama
of cactus in flower, thrusting up
blood-rich entrails glowing on spears
which shiver and sway in the wind off the sea.

And,
and all this world and anti-world,
our truth and mirror-reality,
are inside out
exactly as they were meant to be.